This book belongs to:

____

Made in the USA
San Bernardino, CA
20 April 2020

68408005R00068